MIND ZAPS

SENRYU   PROSE   ILLUSTRATIONS

ALAN PIZZARELLI

HOUSE OF HAIKU

Copyright © 2019 by Alan Pizzarelli

All rights reserved.

First Edition
Printed in the United States of America

ISBN 978-0-9626040-4-1

House of Haiku
Bloomfield, New Jersey
houseofhaiku.com

Cover photograph of Alan Pizzarelli
by Donna Beaver

Book Design by Donna Beaver

House of Haiku Books
by Alan Pizzarelli

Frozen Socks: New and Selected Short Poems
Canary Funeral (limited edition)

"Homer is dead, Dante is dead, Shakespeare is dead, and I'm not feeling so well myself."

    Artemus Ward (1834-1867)

Contents

Dueling Connoisseurs 1
A Fractured Fairytale 9
Senryu Magazine 15
Trailer Trash 51
Breaking News 71
Senryu Samurai 83
Credits 131

Dueling Connoisseurs
A One Act Play

(Dame Benedetto, a wealthy Italian wine connoisseur of eminent repute, invited Signor Biagio Ubriacone, a poet and wine connoisseur widely touted as "The Poet of Oenophilia" to employ his expertise as a guest in her vineyard in the southern region of Italy where upon his arrival he took lodgings in an old edifice on the vineyard. From its appearance, Biagio found Dame Benedetto's vineyard, to be one of those exotic hanging gardens known in an earlier time elsewhere in Italy. Nothing could exceed the intentness with which Biagio examined each and every grape along his path: he sensed a deep intimacy between himself and these grapevine entities. He touched their skin, inhaled their purple scent, and then, after steadily sipping from his flask, held a bunch of unusually large purple grapes in between his legs and sang the Italian drinking song "Bevilo Tutto" as he wrote the following poem):

>   ubriaco
>   lascio che la farfalla
>   indichi la via

>   drunk
>   I let the butterfly lead
>   the way

(Meanwhile, Dame Benedetto, who was envious of his legendary reputation endeavored to give her guest a more habitable air, greeted him with a volume of his poems in hand, as she swung open the front door.)

BENEDETTO: Ah! Signor Ubriacone, benvenuto! Madre di Dio! You look-a so young-a like-a Come sì chiama? Dorian Gray-a!

BIAGIO: Sì, I if only I can buy things on my looks alone.

BENEDETTO: It is a sign that you have come here-a! I prayed to the saints to deliver us-a, the finest poet-a, and connoisseur of wine-a in Italia, and here you are-a, Biagio Ubriacone himself-a!

BIAGIO: Scusi, mi permetta, I was enjoying some grapes from your exquisite vineyard and clumsily stained the crotch of my trousers. It brings to mind a poem I wrote in a vineyard in Tuscani:

> ancora ubriaco
> mi tolgo i pantaloni
> da sopra la testa
>
> drunk again
> pulling my pants off
> over my head

BENEDETTO: Puh-leese-a Signor, you make-a me pee myself-a! Mah — Non c'è problema! I was just reading your latest book of poems-a "Muffa nobile" (Noble Rot), eh questo molto profound-a:

> un altro giorno
> nell'universo   cosa c'è
> per cena?
>
> another day
> in the universe
> what's for dinner?

BIAGIO: Ah! I was eating a rolled spiral of mozzarella cheese and pepperoni, baked and sliced into slender pieces reminiscent of the spiral galaxies and how the universe itself must manga!

BENEDETTO: AH! Come questo?

> finite le scuse
> racconto alla moglie
> del mio rapimento alieno
>
> all excuses spent
> I tell my wife
> about my alien abduction

BIAGIO: Sì, and she believed me!

BENEDETTO: Ma tua moglie Sophia è una donna così bella, sembra che il tuo poema su di lei sia, scusami, umiliante. Come questo?

> quant'era bella
> con i suoi vestiti addosso
>
> how beautiful
> she looked with her clothes on

BIAGIO: Sì, but she was wearing Versace.

BENEDETTO: Vedo! Salute Biagio, taste this vintage, I call-a "Piccole punte trafiletto" Because-a, Calabria is the gnarled toe-a of the Italian boot-a, it is also known as "Cirò," that is high in spirits-a and tannins-a."

(Daintily lifting the glass of wine and holding it up to the sunlit window, Biagio sniffed, swirled the wine and sipped.)

BIAGIO: Ruby red in color, on the nose there is an intense bouquet of volcanic soil and ripe fruits. On the palate it is well structured, soft as a warm summer breeze and very pleasing; a fine Cirò vintage that pairs well with pasta and red sauces.

BENEDETTO: (raising her bushy eyebrow) Ah, well said-a. Here, have some pane to cleanse your palate-a, it is from Giordano the baker-a, you remember Giordano?"

BIAGIO: Sì!, I went to school with him, he was always getting stuck in his school desk and we had to pry him out with lots of lard. He was molto Corpulento!

BENEDETTO: MADRE DI DIO! How he loved to manga!

BIAGIO: Sì, and he used to eat my poems as well, he said it was come sì dice? "Good roughage."

BENEDETTO: Lo so! As fine connoisseurs, we capeesh-a, grey rot-a, can destroy-a crops of grapes-a, when exposed-a, to a climate that is… come sì dice? Moist-a. Here is another vintage to sample. This is-a Prima voce, named for the first tenor in an opera, salute!

BIAGIO: Sì, but grapes, when picked at a timely point during infestation can produce a particularly fine and concentrated sweet vintage. The finest wines are chosen grape by grape. Such are these poems.

(Lifting the fine crystal glass, Biagio then cocked his head and poured the wine into his right ear).

BIAGIO: Ah! It plays a magnificent pastoral symphony of singing wild berries with the rhythmical dun of kettle drums.

(Not to be outdone, Dame Benedetto slowly raised her glass, sunk her nose into it, and proceeded to snort the vintage with both nostrils.)

BENEDETTO: I too hear its music, so sweet-a, so passionate-a! But it also exudes-a, intense-a aromas of fruit pulp-a on the Olfactory nerve-a, followed with warm waves of diminished notes-a on the tonsil-a's, that is, if one still has tonsil-a's.

BIAGIO: Sì, with tonsils it reveals intense aromas of fruit pulp in the throat and nostrils, followed with warm waves of vanilla and haunting diminished notes of dark chocolate on the palate.

BENEDETTO: Signor Biagio, I realize it is late-a and you may be ready to retire for the night-a, but will you please take a moment to sample-a one more vintage, which I have tended in the vineyard-a. It expresses the richness of the Tuscan terroir. I think you will find it, most seductive-a.

(Sipping a mouthful of the vintage and spitting it in her face.)

BIAGIO: Complex and spicy! It explodes on the ears with bold notes that dance a ballet along the palate, followed by a surreal elegance that only Federico Fellini could imagine!

(With that, Biagio wobbled towards the direction of the front door and saying "ciao" then found himself entangled in closet hangers. The next morning, Dame Benedetto found the following poem slipped under her front door):

>   svegliandomi stamane
> sorretto dai rami più alti di un albero
>   non c'è più vino per me

>   woke this morning
> cradled in the upper branches of a tree
>   no more wine for me

❧ Fine ☙

A Fractured Fairytale

Long, long ago, in the Dark Forest, in a land far far away, lived seven dwarfs who worked with a pick-ax and spade, searching for truffles in the heart of the dark forest.

One day, when night had fallen, the masters of the little cottage returned home. Upon a little table stood seven little plates and upon each plate lay a little spoon, besides which there were seven little knives and forks and seven little goblets. Against the wall and side by side, stood (you guessed it, folks) seven little beds covered with seven little clean white sheets.

As they each lit their seven little candles, the first dwarf named Lazy looked around and saw that all seven beds were rumpled, so he said, "Who is this sleeping in our beds?" Then the second dwarf named Sleazy crept closer, saw a beautiful woman

sound asleep, and called the others to come and look at her; "Hi-Ho! Hi Ho!" they sang aloud with surprise.

How frightened she was when she woke and saw seven dwarfs standing at her bedside drooling. But they were very kind and after calming her down

asked what her name was. "My name is Snowflake," she answered.

"And how did you come to get into our cottage?" questioned the dwarfs in harmony. Then she told them how her cruel step-mother had banished her from the kingdom, how the huntsman had spared her life and how she got lost in the Dark Forest until she reached the little cottage.

Then Hop-frog the dwarf said, "If you will cook for us, and make the beds, wash our clothes, mend our socks, sew our buttons, take out the trash, keep everything neat and clean, and maybe go for a roll in the hay with us, then you may stay with us altogether and you shall want for nothing."

"Okay, except for the housework," she answered. And, so she stayed.

"Mirror, mirror upon the wall,
Who is the fairest of all?"
"Thou, O Queen, art the fairest of all — NOT!"

The End

SENRYU MAGAZINE

Number 2

In this Issue

Editor's Introduction
Museum of Senryu Literature Awards
Senryu Toons
Senryu
Featured poet: Haiku Joey Clifton
Book Reviews
Books Received
Across the Editor's Desk
Letters

Editor's Introduction

Senryu is a short poetic genre which focuses on people. Men, women, husbands, wives, children, and relatives. It portrays the characteristics of human beings and the psychology of the human mind. Even when senryu depict living things such as animals, insects, and plant life, or when they depict inanimate objects, they are portrayed with the emphasis on their human attributes.

The senryu can make use of poetic devices such as simile, personification, and metaphor. It can also employ puns, parody, and satire. Unlike haiku, senryu are not reliant on a seasonal or nature reference, but they DO occasionally use them. When they do, it is secondary to the human comedy or drama underlying the poem.

Senryu are not all strictly intended to be humorous. Many senryu express the misfortunes, the hardships, and the woe of humanity.

— Alan Pizzarelli

Museum of Senryu Literature Awards

FIRST PRIZE:

sunrise
"any cock'll do"
crows the capon

        Henny Orpington

SECOND PRIZE:

The fleeing body builders
   turn about suddenly
      and chase back the sea

        W.J. Crockett

THIRD PRIZE:

on Times Square 4 Elvis' hailing cabs

        Carlos Pelvis

HONORABLE MENTION

Chill night
after you the toilet seat
slightly wet

        Everett Threadneedle

empty escalators
go up
and down
so what?!

        Clayton Crutch

SENRYU TOONS

"Remember my haiku
that won first prize in that contest?"
"No, does anyone?!"

SENRYU TOONS

"I'm serious!"
he shouts
wearing a pinwheel hat

SENRYU TOONS

"drool inwardly!"
she mutters to her husband
on the crowded beach

Senryu

I made this with my own hands
says the chef
with eight fingers

        Mario Lemani

between a rock
and a hard place
the geologist

        Orville Dexter

our nosy neighbor
I only talk about
the weather

        Elba Novella

Two men walk into a bar
"My face is up here!"
Says the buxom blonde

        Frankie Fly

home service
the electrician
with the wild hair

    Sophie Wigs

The dentist
Straddles me in the chair —
It was a deep root.

    Brute Fear

high tide
all the bathers
tumble

    Virgil Honeywell

March winds
Oy Vey!
Money wasted on a hair-do

    Mitzi Steinmetz

in the convenience store a long line at the cashier

    Pierce Needleman

mosquito.
that you West Nile?

in the polluted pond a frog croaks

    Redmond Rosehip

at the local zoo
the caged mynah bird
muttering expletives

    Gaston Lipchitz

"Petunias! I found petunias!"
Shouts Aunt Sophie,
then fractures her tibia.

    Tula Mushnick

                        lamp
my husband ducks the   i throw

twilight shrunken clothes tumble in the dryer

hOOters

SL⎯UG

Venus Mons

on a date
the socker player
finally scores

        Fermin Le Pew

After Issa

auto breakdown
who's gonna fix it
you mister cricket?

        Edsel Chase

a sudden thunder storm
cuts off
the evangelist's broadcast

        Tammy Ray Faber

in the tree frog's song strains of "I Got Rhythm"

on the grass hut   a tv antenna

turning on the tv   i go to sleep

        Orville Dexter

  swarming like bees
  around the car's raised hood
  puerto ricans

        Anon.

  5th of july
  the pyrotechnician's clothes
  full of holes

        Luigi Capote

  Missing a kick
  at the dog chewing my dentures
  I wear them anyway

        Jack Merrimack

unhappy vet
I pedal my bike
through poodles

turning to wave
goodbye to her
i walk off the precipice

      Latvia Swift

in the court room
the mime's
mute testimony

      Woody McCarthy

after the trial
the florist comes out
smelling like a rose

      Mitzi Steinmetz

the woodpecker knocks
a wild haired man swings open the door
and slams it shut again

    Etmo Duey

cement pond
a ceramic frog falls in
"made in japan"

    Scovel Landis III

Washing dishes,
washing clothes, wishing...
Everything wishy-washy

    Tao Chang Lee

Fall cleaning
 Sorry spiderweb
— Eeeeek!

    Dusty Blight

Buon appetito!

The vegetarians
sit at the table
by the sunny window

The surgeon orders his steak well
done

Today's Special
is the "Dolly Parton"
two large breasts of chicken

"Dance, snail dance!
Or you're escargot!"
Shouts the chef.

Spilling the flambé
the waiter tries telling a joke
then calls the fire department

                Fryman Cooke

Little Old Man

i used to be
six foot four
says the little old man

"When I was your age..."
he says
then forgets what to say

days are short
so short
I'm still in my pajamas

before bedtime I brush my tooth

69th birthday
a wristwatch tossed
in a drawer of wristwatches

a rooster crows
another old friend
in the obituary

    Benny Fettuccine

Featured Poet: Haiku Joey Clifton

Haiku Joey Clifton. Poet, entertainer & con man extraordinaire – is renowned as the most notorious poet in the anal of modern senryu. Clifton was the Roast Master for the first (and only) Gala haiku Roast, a historic event that has since become an underground legend. However, Clifton's claim that he went to Harvard University is widely disputed as research shows that he only went there to use the men's room. Despite the crotchety critic Rufus Griswald III, who once described him as "brains without purpose," the prominent critic A.J. Pulvertaft noted: "Clifton is unquestionably the worst poet in America, on the other hand, some of his poems are so bad, they're good!"

Clifton, is recognized as the poet laureate of the Blue Lizard Lounge in Las Vegas where he regularly performs singing "intentionally" off-key, followed by a reading of his "haikus." Clifton's poems are a laugh out loud critique of the human condition. Following is our interview with Clifton in his dressing room at the *Blue Lizard Lounge*.

Interview

SM: You call yourself Haiku Joey Clifton, yet your poems are Senryu – Don't you care about that?

JC: Ask me what I think about apathy.

SM: Okay, what do you think about apathy?

JC: I'm glad you asked! I don't care about apathy.

SM: Is it true that you are a master of the Martial arts.

TC: Not exactly, I have a yellow belt.

SM: What's a yellow belt?

TC: When threatened...RUN!

SM: Why do people say you are notorious?

JC: I was once arrested doing stand-up, at a comedy club in Cambridge, a college community.

HM: What for?

JC: I was charged with "Banality" a misdemeanor.

SM: Is that all?

JC: One critic wrote "The audience was so quiet you could hear the zippers in the men's room."

SM: So, what are you up to these days?

JC: Last week I lost my life savings at the race track. Na'aah, I guess betting on a horse named "Lethargic Dancer" was a bad hunch.

**From New & Rejected Poems
by Haiku Joey Clifton (Unpublished)**

>haiku schmiku
>where's my toupee?

>the summer wind
>blows my mother-in-laws perfume
>from across the sea

>bible thumpers
>at my door
>I pray they go away

>fat superman,
>he can still fly
>but not as high

>the homeless man's dog
>poops on the sidewalk
>so does he

Book Reviews

Mr. William Shakespeare's Senryu
by Sy Morehead
Reviewed by Rufus Griswald III

Scribbler's & Sons, London, 2018 (2nd Edition), 231 pp., Hardcover, $23.95.

The notion that not much is known about the life of William Shakespeare is no more than an uneducated myth. In fact, contemporary scholars are revealing more and more about the life and times of Shakespeare, aside from the fact that he spent much of his time fleeing the various plagues of his era in England, often without his pantaloons.

The recent discovery in London of an obscure folio, written in 1607, is the subject of *Mr. William Shakespeare's Senryu,* by Sy Morehead, who makes a very convincing case that an ancient Japanese poetic form, known as *senryu* was written by Shakespeare more than a century before its *origins* in 18th century Japan.

The folio contains 92 poems, most written in three short lines which Mr. Morehead proclaims were penned by "The Immortal Bard of Stratford on Avon" to "amuse poetry enthusiasts at London's Inns of Court & Chancery." He also claims the immortal bard recited some of these short poems at his audition for Ben Jonson's comedy, "Every Man in his Humor" in which authentic playbills list William Shakespeare as one of the "principal comedians."

During his second creative period, 1600-1608 when he wrote his great tragedies, Shakespeare also composed his *comadies*. During those years, it is said that he was so enlightened by poetic brevity, that he reduced his popular play *Hamlet* to the solitary line "To be or not to be, that is the question." At which point, the actor exited the stage for the final curtain. Afterwards, when the proprietor of London's Inns confronted William and asked why *Hamlet* was cut so short, he elegantly sniffed a pinch of snuff, sneezed and responded "vast sails suit not my craft!" and exited stage left. Will's performance at the Court & Chancery was short-lived after being pursued by a torch-bearing mob led by bloodhounds:

> From mine bare buttocks,
> See'st me run —
> O toothy mongrel!

Morehead further claims that Shakespeare lost the infamous folio while fleeing to Warwickshire, following rumors of yet another plague, this one reportedly resulting in permanent hair loss. As portraits and the following poem of the young bard attest, he didn't make it:

> Farewell O youthful mane!
> Cept' in mine nose and ears
> Ere it doth grow long.

Some Elizabethan scholars, however, proclaim that at least some of the short poems dated 1612, were actually written by Marlowe, who was known to own quills, paper and ink. Still, other critics vehemently insist that the author is actually actor/comedian George Burns, who auditioned with Shakespeare for the part of Johannes Shagbab. Burns claimed he didn't pass the audition because at the time he was "too old to play the part" and that it inspired Shakespeare to write the following two-line poem contained in the folio:

> Betrayed by moonlight
> O who can thou trust?

Morehead debunks any claims that Marlowe, Bacon or Burns could have written the folio poems for that matter. However, his statement "How can a slab of bacon possibly write a poem?!" is far from convincing.

In reading *Mr. William Shakespeare's Senryu,* the question remains: Did the Immortal Bard of Stratford on Avon really write these verses?

Morehead points out that in the original folio, some of the verses are initialed J.S., which he claims is a pseudonym (Johannes Shagbab) Shakespeare used for some of his more controversial senryu.

Under the pseudonym of Shagbab, Shakespeare also ridiculed the current fashion trend:

> How oddly suited!
> One too many plumes
> In thy pointed hat!

Perhaps, the most convincing of Morehead's claim is one senryu dedicated to Ann Hathaway:

> Ere long the sagging clouds
> Hast given likeness to thy bosoms
> O droppeth it!

The Monkey's Underwear
by Archibald Parrot
Reviewed by Teddy Attenborough

Fruit of the Loom Books, 2018, 970 Roadrunner Way, Santa Fe, NM 87501, 150 pp., Clothbound, $9.95.

In his fourth collection of Senryu, Archibald Parrot once again displays his faculties of wit and acute imagination, which have given us such classics as *Madame Bovine*, *Of Mice & Midgets*, and, *The Turtle's Toupee*.

As in his previous books, Parrot accomplishes this by implementing the poetic device of anthropomorphism: ascribing human form or attributes to a nonhuman thing or being. In doing so, the animals, plants, insects, etc., are portrayed with vivid human characteristics. Thus, an aggregation of carpenter termites are characterized as Union Protesters picketing the hiring of an aardvark; an ordinary otter eating oysters can possess the distinctive characteristics of a gay Englishman enjoying a can of spotted dick. Whatever the strength of Mr. Parrot's anthropomorphism lies not only in its correlative traits but in its unabashed truthfulness.

> Grazing sheep
> gossip
> about the new farmhand

Hit-or-Miss Press, has announced the publication of **Desert Doldrums** — The Humdrum Poems of Sterling Foster.
Reviewed by Hart Copperfield

Considered by many to be the most irksome poet of our time, Foster's dull and often dreary doggerel evoke the irrepressible urge to yawn, hence the unpopularity of his work (with the exception of a large number of effete insomniacs). Here is such an example:

> this evening stillness
> a moment of moonlight
> followed by silence

Foster was fond of silence, undoubtedly because he was endowed with enormous ears and would often say things like "Let those who are taking issue with my poetry know that I can hear them." Later, Foster became a Buddhist monk, who in his "new style" of poetry celebrated weariness:

> nothing special happening today
> buddha's birthday

These poems, it will be noted, contain no capital letters; the poem is wholly given up to the lower case. However, like his earlier work, it denotes the same lack of sensibility, which can be interpreted as Foster's modest way of alluding to himself as bald and overweight.

Unfortunately, time did not allow Foster to furnish more of these new-style poems, which are unquestionably the more interesting selections in this tedious text.

Pigeons All Over The Place
by Hilda Mockingbird
Reviewed by Prof. Hildegard Bundy

One hundred and one distinctive, lyrical bird poems. 72 pp., 7x5 inches. $10 postpaid from the author at Studio B, 13 Hummingbird Lane, Countryside, VA 24592.

Ever the one to share her love for birds, poet, and ornithologist Hilda Mockingbird has delighted us over the years with books such as *Bird's O'Clock, The Flying Cage*, and her award-winning novella, *For Whom The Birds Troll*.

In her latest and best book to date, Mockingbird focuses her keen observation on the birds of urban slums and the beat of the inner city:

>   in the ghetto
>   masked sparrows
>   fighting

Many of these poems have accented vowel movements and when reading aloud, have the rhythmic beat of Rap.

As such, these poems work best as an oral form, usually with someone making clicking, popping and sucking sounds with mouth and hands, as a background:

> piles of poop
> on the stoop,
> gotta pigeon coop say what?

With a spread of wings and melodious song, Hilda Mockingbird continues to enrich our lives with her keen perception and bird's eye view of the world.

Books Received

One Hundred Farts by Hideki Soto. Jushitsu Press, 2018, P.O. Box 9153, 1-chome, Osaka-fu, Japan, 116 pp., softcover, no price given. Sample:

> Having eaten all the leftovers
> I win the farting contest

Made You Look by Marcy Gould. Made You Look Books 2019, Clearview Elementary School, 5th Ave. & 6th St., Boresville, ID, 83500, 50 pp., hardcover $14.95. Sample:

> a fallen leaf
> is coming back to the branch
> made you look! made you look!

The Senryu Handbook: How to Write Senryu and Do the Charleston by J.W. Pulvertaft. Illustrated by Arthur Murray. Charles Scribbler's & Sons, 2019, 231 pp., $89.95.

> ballroom dancing
> the man
> with two left feet

The Sheen of Linoleum by Dusty Blight, Cleanhome Keepers Press 2018, 100 pp., $10.00. Sample:

> after i wax
> the kitchen floor
> the dog runs in place

Across the Editor's Desk

The Association of Athletic Supporters announces the 2019 Senryu competition. Deadline: October 31, 2019. For rules SASE to Assn. of Athletic Supporters, P.O. Box 2187, Scrotum, New Jersey 07222.

Ditter Oostdyk, Professor, Faculty of Senryu Literature, Random University, was the recipient of a Zoologists Foundation Fellowship Grant in 2018 for his book *A Yak in Trousers.*

A new Anthology of Senryu is being planned by co-editors Chic Peckham and Desmond Gluck, Jr., titled *The Hen Who Came To Dinner,* will be published by Raw Egg Press. Senryu and related forms plus pertinent articles will be considered.

Book Awards

The Demerit Book Awards for the worst books published in 2018-2019 have been announced as follows.

First Prize
Sydell Oglethorpe, *Featherless Geese,* Press This, La Crosse, Wisconsin, 2018.

Second Prize
Benet Bouffant, *The Poodle's Pompadour*, Four Paws Press, Mutland, Vermont, 2018.

Third Prize
Brushrod Wilcox, Editor, *The Selected Political Haiku of Spiro T. Agnew*, nolo contendere press, Cockeysville, Maryland, 2019. Judges: Rod Specius (chairman), Nathan Fink and some unknown Frenchman.

Letters

CALL OF PRAISE

Wow! I read through the entire issue (SM: No. 1) in one sitting. The poems were boisterously merry and made me chortle. Thank you for the thought-provoking articles, which I plan to share with my parrots.

> Hilda Mockingbird
> Countryside, VA

ANOTHER SOURCE

Thumbing through the pages of Senryu Magazine Number One, I laughed so hard that I wrenched the muscles in my neck and could only speak properly with the aid of a ventriloquist's dummy. Unfortunately, I was still called for jury duty.

> Woody McCarthy
> Live Oak, FL

HOLIER-THAN-THOU?

As a God-Fearing Church-goer, I find your magazine morally offensive. Do you realize that in Japan, SM can only be sold wrapped in brown paper at adult bookstores in the red light district of Osaka?!

> Sister Mary Crucifix
> Newark, NJ

Editor's response: How'd you find out?

BORSCHT BELT

Clark Schnabel's review of Fryman Cooke's *Tender is the Chicken* (SM: No. 1), was deliciously insightful and well done.

I also found J.W. Pulvertaft's "Suggestions for Writing Senryu," full of perspicacity with the exception of suggestion #9, "Eat a lot of low-fat yogurt."

How ridiculous. Everyone knows that borscht is more conducive.

> Hannah Halvah
> Catskill, NY

SOMETHING TO CHEW ON

Although I found J.W. Pulvertaft's article "Suggestions for Writing Senryu" (SM: No. 1) informed, intelligent, and well written, he failed to fully elucidate the following drills: Always punctuate, when applying Caps. Avoid fillings and extract unnecessary words. In addition, sentimentalism will often render a senryu unpalatable. I have also found that a good whiff of N20, makes senryu even funnier.

> Brute Fear D.D.S.
> Bronx, NY

SCUTTLE REBUTTAL

In his essay " The Art of Rigid Configuration" (SM: No. 1), Kent Scuttle persists beating a dead horse, presumably because it has four legs. I, therefore, take this auspicious occasion and highly recommend that he rid himself of the 5-7-5 form like a pair of old socks, of which I am sure in his case is number 17.

> Kitty Lickliter
> Altoona, PA

VIVA MAMMA !

Congratulations on another great issue!

> Love,
> Mamma

p.s. Did you enjoy the veal parmigiana I mailed you?

TRAILER TRASH

The Letters of Etmo Duey

bitter morning
neighbors sittin' together
without any teeth

deer maw,

i applied for a job as a short order cook at the "sizzling steaks".

i nose im not so short, but i applied anyhow. anyways, on the application where it sez "what is yr ambition" i wrote in: "to cook sizzling steaks." i think that should land me the job.

yr big boy,
etmo

    from the sink
    piled high with dirty dishes
    i pick one that's almost clean

    sick of eating spam
    i turn on the pc,
    more god damn spam!

deer maw,

flo was walkin' to the laundry mat
yesterday when she cum face to face
with a huge green creature, with "big
red eyes" n' well she just flat out
fainted. when she cum to, she noticed
her new salvation army coat wuz full
of large holes — must be that damn moth
man again!

yr baby boy,
etmo.

    unable to afford
    a fly swatter
    we adopt a stray cat

    as I write
    on my lap top
    the cat plays with the mouse

    the cat does a soft march
    on my big beer belly
    then the lil' fucker pukes!

    christmas eve
    I light the Yule log
    on tv

    new years day
    a strand of tinsel   dangles
    from the cat's ass

dear maw,

i aint callin' cousin mary beth jo bob
ugly, but when she cries, its mighty
strange how the tears roll down her
backside.

yr lovin' son,
etmo

    after sex
    she paints her eyebrows
    back on her face

    she farts
    n' its o.k.
    i burp n' she sez
    i'm disgusting
    go figger.

deer maw,

flo iz feelin' much better tho she's
filled our trailer with moth balls n'
wont turn on the lights.

i keep slippin' on dem dang balls
but dey sure make our place smell
nice.

yr sonny boy,
etmo

    dere goes that mouse again
    the cat
    no longer gives a shit

deer maw,

i nose i been out of work a spell.
,n' y'nose I been a'tryin' -
now the news is an asteroid,
"large enough to wreak worldwide
destruction," is headed towards the
earth at 60,000 mph and is due to
strike this fall."
so why bother?!

yr boy,
etmo

ps: hears five bucks for groceries.
sorry i can't give more cuz i ran out
of beer.

    thought i smelt
    vegetable soup
    but it was just me

    the cat turns its nose up
    at the leftovers
    n' licks its ass

deer maw,

my good buddy, call him mutt cuz i dont no his name. anyways, mutt is a beer chuggin' tattoo artist – but for sum reason he dont do tattoos no more. he worked at the pet store in town but got his ass fired the first day – i guess putting the gerbils in with the snakes was a bad idea – now he's stuffin' road kill n' sells 'em, its called taxi dermee – anyways, i bought one dat wuz all mashed up n' shit – but i agree with mutt it does makes a kewl conversation piece.

yr "little bunny",
etmo

    misplacing her glasses
    the hoarder
    finds another pair

trailer park picnic
every one of the fat lady's pomes
mention food

in her pants
ants ants ants

picking his nose
one of our neighbors
tells us what he likes to eat

after pronouncing
the prune pie "delicious"
he shits his pants

deer maw,

I'm shure u 'member da time when I
wuz a boyscout for troupe 72.

Dat time when u sent me off on dat
mountain retreat. I's sure u well
member how dat kind camp counseler
drove me back home a day later with
a dried-up shitload steamin' in
ma pants. Well, like I told ya back
then den, dem dang scout masters
told us scary stories bout dis crazy
mary lady, who wore a wedding gown
n' liked to chop up boy scouts into
little pieces with an axe. Well,
needless to say, none of us boyz s
went outside the cabin to use the
outhouse, which was a good 30 yards
into the woods.

Yr little stinky,
Etmo

    even when i walk
    against the wind, the stink of
    my fart   stays

deer maw,

flo's been feedin' dis'ol stray
dawg, so i sided to take the mutt
in. he's a scruffy lookin' mongrel,
slobberin' all over da god damn place
n' he sneezes a lot 2 -- so's i calls
him "disease" -- aint dat a hoot?!
anyhows, he makes a good playmate for
our cat.

yr boy,
etmo

Ps: Dere he goes again with the cat
in his jaws.

    at my trailer door
    the bible ladies act like
    they never seen a man nekkid

deer maw,

today, when i was huntin' squirrels in
the back woods,i met dis geeologiest
fella -dey study rocks & hard stuff-
so's i asks this fella "how do rocks
grow?" n' he laughs & sez "that's the
dumbest question i ever heard, rocks
don't grow!" so i sez "well then, if
yr so smart, how do they get so big?!"
-- & walked away. guess dat gave him
sumtin to think about!

yr pride n' joy,
etmo.

    the string beans I planted,
    never sprouted
    sow be it

Deer sun,

Cuzzin' Lumpy writ me today askin bout cha. Hairs a letter he axed me to sen to ya. I nose Lumpy is kind of a bad seed but he's still family. Gotta go cause I got a opossum on the fire.

Luv,
Yr ma.
(Letter encloseted)

"Howdy Cuzzin Etmo,
Sheet! Las time a sawz ya wuz wen
I wuz in dipers – I member I was 18
at da time. Anyhows, sorey fr not
keepin' in touch. Sure u heard bout
my prison sentence for bank robbery
– I nose it was kinda dumb to ask
the securiti gard fr permission. –
dats what I gets for being polite,
y'nose, non-killin'-like – next
thing I nose, I got a gun stickin'
in my ear. Anyhoo, I's plum pleased
as moonshine dat yr a publist poet!
I alwaze news, youz waz smart
havin' gradiated 8h grade n'all."

Yr cuzzin, Lumpy
PS: watcha think about dis pome I
writ:

    a mosquito
    bites me
    I smash its @#*+&%! head

Cuz,

Dats a knee slapping poem you writ
dere Lump. Better den any thang
I writ. Gotta go, Flo is plucking
chickens n' they aint kilt yet -- we
gots all deez featherless chickens
cluckin in the coop. gotta go.

Etmo

Hi cuzin Etmo,

Sorri, I dint writ 4 a spell ubt I wuz in need of sum cash n' and signed up to be a boxing sparing partner for Bone Smasher Smith. As I writ u dis letter from my hospital bed, I now unnerstan' how he gots his name. Gotta go now, they're cutting off the body cast dis afternoon.

yr cuz,
Lumpy

deer maw,

i hopes yr sittin' down cuz I gots
some sad news — our lil'pussycat
fell dead. Poor thang was stiff as a
board when I finally founds it in da
kitchin buried under some stuff. I
thunk I smelt sumtin' reekin' for the
past couple months. Then, uncle mutt
stopt by a'vsititn, n' he noticed
the foul smell before he even come
inside. I sd I thought so n' when we
found the puss I was glad it wasn't
Flo, who I hadn't seen around for
a spell. Anyhow, wez dug a hole n'
buried da lil critter in its litter
box, which it never used no way, n'
it brought a tear to my eye to see
our dog diseases help diggin' the
grave.

yr one & only,
etmo duey

ps: Cuzin' Lumpy iz in the hospital
again.

    took a short cut
    through the cow pasture
    my shoes grow'd 3 times bigger

Deer son,

Jus got back home from dumpster divin' for groceries. how many times I gotta tell ya to not walk thru the cow pasture?

Yr Ma,

ps: that reminds me bout sumtin' I writ when u wuz my baby boy

    told he's the daddy
    the milk man
    in a bad moo'd

deer maw,

thanks for yr litter.
i nose flo cusses like a truck driver
after all, she wuz one - at least she
don't cuss out loud during church
services anymore, so she's been
tryin' to hold her tongue. it's a
fuckin' hard habit to break.

yr little scar head,
etmo

    end of the month
    time to take a bath

BREAKING NEWS

in the confessional
the pedophile priest
is again given absolution

with tiki torches
white supremacists march
without any hoods

the war hero
returns home
to his bickering family

Asking the little boy
"What do you want to be
 when you grow up?"
 "A girl!"

always with a smile
the young man
who hanged himself

trying
to console the bride
the matchmaker

after scolding
her spoiled child
she buys him a new toy

the visiting guests
sit quietly
with their smartphones

the old musician
picks up his guitar and sings
the me-too blues

the incestuous child
takes the family secret
to her grave

the dumpster diver
returns to the abandoned house
with her groceries

the atheist
looks up at the heavens
and shrugs

at the wedding reception
the couple having an affair
act like strangers

in the cracked picture frame
her ex

waking again
in his jail cell
the murderer's nightmare

birds migrate
over the Mexican border
and the children in cages

global warming
   a coffin   slowly floats   down the street

court testimony
the rape victim
abused again

1960's Abortion

a woman
bends a wire coat hanger —
the bathwater turns red

school's out —
students run with hands
clasped over their heads

driving
the fire truck
a face of scars

After Ryōkan

the thief took it too
the moon
at my window

SENRYU SAMURAI
川柳侍

Toshiro Shokan was a samurai warrior who on a whim, in 1789 left his hermitage in Edo and traveled across Japan seeking peace, friends and senryu poetry. Legend has it that he grew weary of war and sought a new life as a poet wanderer.

Senryu Samurai is one of the records of his journey.

The first day of the seventh moon, Mt. Fuji shrouded in mist. Climbed ten chō uphill only to climb ten more chō.

Will it never end?

Chō: approx. 120 yards

Crossing mustard fields asked the way of a farmer who, pointing a long daikon was helpful — Truly, a man of zen — who kindly lent us his horse, saying "when you arrive in Senju, write down the first thing you see and send it back to me with the horse."

Daikon: Japanese radish

On our way, visited the No-No Kimono Shrine — My companion, Shino, said "The Emperor of the deity here — used to wear backless kimonos. Tale behind it common knowledge."

2.

Crossed vale of Senju on thirteenth of the seventh moon — anticipation mounting — finally caught sight of a village in drizzling rain and made for it.

Later wrote down the first thing I saw in the village.

物干にまわし掛けあり春の雨

mawashi hung on a wash line – spring rain

I tied it on the horse's saddle and with a slap on its rear — sent it off trotting back to the mustard farmer.

Mawashi: the loincloth that a sumo wrestler wears.

3.

Spent the night at the ramshackle hermitage of Osai, a sumo wrestler, poet, and master of the I-Chow, who invited us to judge the evening Uta-awase, a contest party where teams of local merchant poets compete composing poems on a variety of topics.

Well-to-do, Osai did his best to entertain us, even though he broke his toes when he dropped the braised oxen he was eating and appointed me to select the three winning poems.

1st prize:

隣り合う雑魚寝の力士鼾に屁

> side by side
> sumo wrestlers sleeping
> snoring and farting
>
> Hikarido

2nd prize

唐辛子食えば火を噴く背の牡丹

> eating red peppers
> the peonies behind me
> burst into flames
>
> Osai

3rd prize

女郎花あなたに立てり根を見せつ

the maiden flower stands there roots exposed

> Hiroaki Aso

4.

Judging the contest was quite a task from moonlight to dawnlight.

六千の句を選すれど柿皆無

checking 6,000 poems
not one persimmon

5.

Next morning set off on horseback and followed a foot-worn path winding downhill through mountain woods under a red sun — faint scent of salt breezes from the coastland — past a narrow river where we caught sight of a woman bathing by a trickling waterfall. My eyes could not avert her beauty as we rode along the river bank.

6.

All night tossing in bed, could not stop thinking of the young woman bathing in the falls until the morning light —

Tired set off through dense mountain forest under rolling thunder of dark clouds — Shino, a haikai poet, riding ahead of me turned and recited a hike:

はたたがみ馬の耳垂れ雨滂沱

> *rolling thunder*
> *the horses ears bent down*
> *in the pouring rain*

Hearing this, I laughed and yelled, "Ha!" pointing out that the words "rolling thunder" could be added to any hike. Such as:

古池や蛙飛び込むはたたがみ

> *old pond*
> *a frog jumps in*
> *rolling thunder*

Up ahead, Shino nodded and shouted back:

閑さや岩が吸い込むはたたがみ

> *quiet*
> *the rock absorbing*
> *rolling thunder*

7.

Spent night at Soka — bathed and bedded down
in a nearby field. Next morning under blue skies —
Shino and I packed up and sloshed thru slippery
marshlands — poking with long sticks — here
and there — later arrived at the post town, hired
fresh horses before fishing in the nearby village of
Namazu.

8.

振りむけば眼前にある馬の尻

suddenly turning around
my face in the hindquarters
of a horse

9.

That night, Shino said "the poet Namazu who was born here and took his name from this village was haunted all his life by nightmares of yodeling fish heads." Here are two of his poems I recall:

兜煮に腹の張りくる最後っ屁

> The great fish head
> becomes a bloated belly
> and then a deadly gas.

鵜飼せし夢から覚めて息詰まる

Dreamt
I was a cormorant fishing
woke up choking.

10.

On a narrow path along the seacoast, trees oozing with red moss — crossed a rope bridge under chilly skies — high mountains mopped with swirling clouds. At post town of Muro-no-Yashima, visited Henjen Bunpitsu, a pioneer of erotic senryu from Yoshiwara who housed as many as 40 concubines and asked the same question each evening when he arrived home, "Okay, who hasn't got a headache?"

He later established a cultural circle and published a periodical: Sekushī na (sexy), which included erotic sketches, senryu, critical articles and a geisha of the month foldout.

祭りにて女に目配せ我螢

at a festival I wink at the ladies
I'm that kind of firefly.

前戯には時間がないよゴジラさん

no time for foreplay, Godzilla!

芋の皮剥いて彼女の尻思い

peeling potatoes, recalling her buttocks.

女下手川柳好みの我と記せ

write me down
as one who loved senryu,
and loose women.

Henjen Bunpitsu

11.

From the house of Bunpitsu — traveled along the marshland roads — without horse or mule Shino and I took turns on the back of each other on the windblown trail — turned north at the caverns and plodded on to Imaichi.

Reaching the village, we finally found the hut of Odo Keta at the side of the mountain. Odo Keta, a disciple of Bunpitsu, wrote zany senryu with a twist.

寝室で押し突きうめく配達夫

> thrusting and moaning
> in the bedroom
> the delivery men

12.

Toenails grown long — mended holes in my tatami. Feet aching — burnt them with moxa and next day started fresh — nine days of blistering heat and lashing rain. Worn out — finally reached the house of Sensei Aso Fugawari in Nikko. Fugawari, a rich merchant who owned the local Fuzake (Lampoon) Newspaper who published his views in a daily column.

Born into a wealthy family of merchants — an eccentric of the highest order whose notorious antics are legendary in Japan. He often imposed his views on others by twisting their noses until they cried "ojisan!" (uncle).

彼の妻のどもる涙の流れ際

on the verge of tears, his stuttering wife.

Moxa: healing powder

13.

Left the house of Fugawari the following afternoon with Shino who with a sore red nose plodded on into the farmlands of the poet Bukiyo at the foot of Mt. Kurokami. B' a bumbling country bumpkin whose clumsiness is a village legend.

Once, he accidentally used gun powder while preparing a meal of stuffed bamboo for a wedding celebration.

水転げ我も転げる岩の上

where the water
tumbles over the rocks
so do I.

ぎこちない五日目我が骨打ち痛み

my bones
feel the bruises
a clumsy day.

14.

Took the boat at Iwanua — to visit the gravestone of Kaai Fufuie — a poor merchant poet of the Kyushi Province. Fufuie had crossed eyes, which caused him to purchase two of everything from the local merchants. Encouraged by Akubi Osuru, the local dog groomer — Fufuie learned the poetic form Maekuzuke from Odo Keta, a pupil of Bunpitsu. He later became the founding editor of the magazine, Warai Iwashi (Laughing Sardine).

Maekuzuke 前句付け

小言妻戻りて「そしてもう一つ！」

> after scolding her husband
> the wife returns
> "and one more thing!"   Fufuie

かくて恋なり
かくて恋なり

> and so love goes
> and so love goes   old saying

Fufuie's poems are mostly satirical and often irreverent:

「夫婦して共に髭あり」と写真屋の声

> the photographer mutters
> "both have whiskers,"
> his wife…. too."

15.

Crossing the bridge in Kasashimai — home of poet Kinshi Manuke — who studied for years to become a genetic scientist — but gave it up to start a lobster farm and study senryu under the tutelage of Iwashi.

Spent a few days at the local inn where Manuke was well known. The following verse is said to have been written by Manuke while fleeing in his underwear —

大伊勢海老前垂れ掛けて行く畳

a giant lobster
wearing a bib
runs over the tatami.

16.

Near Taga Castle — after hearing the faint sounds of children playing — I was unexpectedly arrested — as a "spy" by a commander of the feudal lord named Yoshimori.

敵陣より砂糖壺借り何想う

>borrowing a cup of sugar
>from the enemy camp
>what was i thinking?

戦場の真上に無情の三日月や

how merciless
a crescent moon
over the battlefield

尋問の頬打ちの毎梅を愛で

every other time
the interrogator slaps my face
i admire the plum blossoms

17.

Up all night — I devised a clever plan:

草木の名聞き訪ね野に逃げる

> asking the names
> of plants and trees
> i escape into the fields

深深と山篭もりして酒飲まん

now that i have taken shelter
deep in the mountains
why should i not drink sake?

沼に落ちなお疎ましい姑かな

sinking in the swamp
even now i hate to think
of my mother-in-law

洞穴にいざる我に無情の潮

crawling safely into a cave
the tide rushes in
not caring how i feel

流れ着き腐れかかった柿を食べ

washed ashore
i eat a persimmon
not wholly rotten

18.

Lips parched — beat and skeleton weary — stumbled upon a small pond — drank deep and passed out — woke hours later when the sunset shown through my eyelids.

糞垂れの我見る蛙古き池

> a frog looks at me
> as i take a dump
> by the old pond

19.

After much rest — set off along an old dirt road and as luck would have it — flagged down a farmer driving horse and cart who kindly took me to a nearby town.

Finally arrived at the town of Shiogama — wishing me well the farmer gave me a silver coin and drove off down the road.

With silver coin — headed straight for the local izakaya bar — where I found a kindred spirit with the proprietor named Kaji who knew of a couple of poets — I mentioned during my long journey.

20.

Next morning arrived at Kaji's house to find him singing an Italian Opera in a pink tutu — following that — we sat and talked on a wide range of topics while snacking from a bowl of deep-fried sushi.

He also kept a caged bird — a white dove that would make a laughing sound at certain points of our conversation — it seemed as if the bird understood — and was mocking some of our opinions.

After a fine meal of raw egg, miso soup and shoots — set off at sunset with Kaji — who took me to a grove of cherry blossoms — strolling on the winding path of small white stones — swept by the sensation as if walking on heavenly clouds.

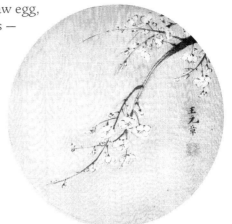

It was then — I saw seated in a passing rickshaw
the face of the woman I saw many moons ago —
bathing in the falls on the road to Senju.

Gob-smacked, I asked Kaji if he knew who she is?
"Her name is Tosembo," she is the only daughter of
the shogun of this prefecture. She too is a poet — so
perhaps she would welcome meeting you.

21.

Just before dawn — Kaji arrived with two horses — and we rode to the imperial palace where he instructed me to wait in a garden of camellias.

The glossy pink-gold sheen of the flowers in the dawning light thrilled me with a sensation never felt before. At that moment — a voice behind me spoke, saying — "The leaves make tea and the seeds an oil — the Camellia is the flower of perfect love."

Looking up — I bowed low before the beauty of Tosembo dressed in a lovely kimono. Our eyes meeting — I was struck — by the thunderbolt of Shinjitsu no koi (True Love).

It was at that moment — Kaji came running out of the palace — shouting — "the warriors of Yoshimori are coming, the warriors of Yoshimori are coming!"

突撃の刀の音の五月蠅さよ

charging into battle
how annoying
the clatter of swords

日が暮れて敵を矢で突く我疲れ

as the day darkens
i'm just seeing if i tire
impaling the enemy with arrows

戦果てて村人踊る蜂の巣や

war over
thought the villagers were doing a dance
broken beehive

ほととぎす戦場静かに木魂して

the call of a hototogisu
echoes
across the silent battlefield

Toshiro Shokan

侍が刀を置きて一句成す

the samurai
puts down his sword
and writes a poem

Tosembo

Credits

Many of the works in this book are new and are published here for the first time. The author is grateful to the following publications where some of these poems first appeared: *Rainsong* (Haiku Northwest/Vandina Press, 2014); Bottle Rockets Press, Simply Haiku/Senryu and Prune Juice.

All poems by fictional authors written by Alan Pizzarelli.

Note: The haiku poems in this book are printed in *italics*.

Italian translations
from *Dueling Connoisseurs*
by Luca Cenisi

Japanese translations
from *Senryu Samurai*
by Emiko Miyashita

"Senryu Samurai" title
"mawashi"
"side by side"
"eating red peppers"
"the maiden flower"
"checking 6,000 poems"
"rolling thunder"
"old pond"
"quiet"
"suddenly turning around"
"the great fish head"
"dreamt I was"
"a giant lobster"
"maekuzuke"
"the samurai"

Japanese translations
from *Senryu Samurai*
by Yuko Otomo

"write me down"
"on the verge of tears"
"where the water"
"my bones"
"at a festival"
"thrusting and moaning"
"the photographer mutters"
the call of a hototogisu"
"charging into battle"
"as the day darkens"
"how merciless"
"now that I have taken shelter"
"borrowing a cup of sugar"
"every other time"
"asking the names"
"sinking in the swamp"
"crawling safely into a cave"
"washed ashore"
"a frog looks at me"
"war over"

Photographs and Illustrations
Drawings by Alan Pizzarelli: 33, 51, 81
Photographs and Illustrations by Donna Beaver: 22, 34

from *A Fractured Fairytale*
Illustrator unknown (Treasury of Well-Loved Tales, digitized by the Internet Archive with funding from Kahle/Austin Foundation).

from *Senryu Samurai*
Public Domain Ukiyo-e illustrations. Ukiyo-e translates as "picture[s] of the floating world" and is a genre of

Japanese woodblock prints and paintings that flourished from the 17th through 19th centuries.

Mizuno Toshikata: 83
Katsushika Hokusai: 84, 104
Tsukioka Yoshitoshi: 85, 88, 109, 110, 112, 129
Konoshima Okoku: 86
Jokata Kaiseki: 86
Hasui Kawase: 87
Utagawa Kuniyoshi: 87, 106, 119, 128
Utagawa Kunisada: 89, 90, 100, 104
Kawase Hasui: 92, 111, 117
Tomioka Eisen: 93
Hashiguchi Goyo: 94
Keisai Eisen: 96
Utagawa Hiroshige: 97, 113, 120
Nishimura Shigenaga: 98
Mori Tetsuzan: 99
Goyō Hashiguchi: 102
Shuntei Katsukawa: 103
Tsuchiya Koitsu: 108
Ohara Koson: 111
Torii Kiyomine: 114
Watanabe Seitei: 115
Teisai Hokuba: 116
Takahashi Hiroaki: 118
Isen'in Hoin Eishin: 120
Unkown: 121
Kawarazaki Shodo: 122
Igawa Sengai: 123
Katsukawa Shuntei: 124, 125, 126
Utagawa Toyokuni: 127

Deep bow to Emiko Miyashita, Yuko Otomo, and Luca Cenisi for their translations.

Special thanks to Donna Beaver who made this book possible.

About the Author

Alan Pizzarelli began writing short poems in the late 1960s. In 1971, he started attending meetings of the Haiku Society of America in New York City and studied haiku and related forms under the tutelage of Professor Harold G. Henderson, author of *An Introduction to Haiku* (Doubleday) and *Haiku in English* (Charles Tuttle).

Since then, his classic original English language haiku and senryu have received worldwide acclaim and popularity. Pizzarelli is a pioneer of English-language senryu and a leading literary spokesman for the American haiku and senryu movement.

His poetry has appeared in a variety of textbooks, periodicals, and anthologies, including *Handbook of Poetic Forms* (Teachers & Writers Collaborative, New York, 1987); *Haiku*, edited by Czesław Miłosz (Wydawnictwo, Kraków Poland, 1992); *Haiku Moment* (1993) and *How to Haiku* (2002), edited by Bruce Ross, published by Tuttle Publishing; *Haiku World: An International Poetry Almanac*, edited by William J. Higginson (Kodansha International Ltd., 1996); *The Haiku Handbook* by William J. Higginson with Penny Harter (McGraw-Hill, 1985; Kodansha International, 25th Anniversary Ed., 2013); *Mirrors & Windows: Connecting with Literature, Level IV* (EMC Publishing, 2009); *Baseball Haiku*, edited by Cor van den Heuvel (W.W. Norton, 2007); and in all three editions of *The Haiku Anthology* edited by Cor van den Heuvel (Doubleday, 1974; Simon & Schuster, 1986; W.W. Norton, 1999).

Pizzarelli was a consultant for *Jack Kerouac's Book of Haikus* edited by Regina Weinreich (Penguin Poets, 2003). From 2005-2009 he was also the senryu poetry editor for the online journal, Simply Haiku. His latest book, *Frozen Socks* (House of Haiku) is a comprehensive collection of his selected short poems from 1969 to 2015.

Alan Pizzarelli is co-host and co-producer of the podcast *Haiku Chronicles* <haikuchronicles.com>.

Made in the USA
Middletown, DE
14 February 2020